TO KANSAS CITY AND THE GRANDBABIES
OF DAN AND T.L.B. MAY YOU NEVER FORGET
YOU ARE CROWNED.

Grab Your Crown

KRISTA BOAN

illustrations by

ALYSIA QUISENBERRY

load the van
and head downtown

singing, cheering
confetti spray

dancing horses
big parade

Glitter and gold
a sea of blue

We've known days
when skies looked dark
when skies looked dark

opponents big
so strong, so smart

We never gave up
played hard to the end
and the very last swing
often brought a win

We're all players
a royal team

ROYALS

where character counts and love is supreme

Thirty years from now
if the lights grow dim

your opponents too strong
your chances too slim

Remember your crown

claim victory

the battle is won

for those who believe

sleepy eyes
dreams of fun

hold your crown tight
victory's won

ROYALS

Hold on to what you have so that no one will take your crown.

REVELATION 3:11

Made in the USA
Charleston, SC
19 April 2016